Create
WISH

Using
A candle, a crystal
&
the imagination
of your
MIND

Robert W. Wood D.Hp
(Diploma in Hypnotherapy)

Rosewood Publishing

First published in U.K. 2001
By Rosewood Publishing
P.O. Box 219, Huddersfield,
West Yorkshire HD2 2YT

www.rosewood-gifts.co.uk

Revised cover and
Re-printed in 2011

Copy-editing
Margaret Wakefield BA (Hons) London
www.euroreportage.co.uk

Cover photograph by
Andrew Caveney BA (Hons)
www.andrewcaveneyphotography.co.uk

Cover and layout re-designed by
AJ Typesetting
www.ajtype.co.uk

Printed in Great Britain by
Delta Design & Print Ltd
www.deltaleeds.co.uk

ISBN 978-0-9532930-2-5   BK3 oOo

The key to happiness is having dreams.
The key to success is making dreams come true.

oOo

A wish

The feeling or expression of a desire or a hope for the future, either concerning your own or someone else's welfare, health, wealth, energy, luck, or piece of mind.

Wish fulfilment

The mechanism involving the release of tension, brought about by re-enacting in fantasy a situation in which a goal is attained.

A kit

A set of tools, supplies etc. for use together for a purpose.

A candle

Have you ever lit a candle for a prayer or to make a wish, be it in the privacy of your own home or in a church? It may have been just for decorative purposes, perhaps whilst having an evening meal, to create a romantic feeling. For whatever reason, have you ever noticed that within a few moments of the candle being lit, there seems to be a sense of calm, peace; a comfortable feeling being experienced? If you have, then you are already aware of the magic and wonder of candle-burning.

What is there about a simple flame that can exercise such a strong psychological, often almost magical effect on us? It's as if its bright light awakens an 'inner light' within us, and for that moment banishes the darkness of our deepest fears, our doubts and our worries.

The ancient saints, priests and magicians have all lit candles to help make wishes or prayers come true. Candles being lit for these purposes are the cornerstone of all the main religions.

oOo

A light will show you the way
And fill you with happiness.

oOo

Crystals

Crystals and Gemstones have always been highly prized for their beauty, their ability to help attract good luck and fortune and their healing powers, as well as their mystical, spiritual like properties.

It seems that healers, shamans, priests and spiritual seekers have been attracted to these special powers since the dawning of time - powers that seem to inspire, delight, and capture the imagination.

The mind

The entity in an individual responsible for thought, feelings and speech, having the faculty of original or creative thought. Houses the subconscious: that part of the mind considered to be outside or only partly within one's conscious awareness, and the place where the imagination can be found.

The imagination

The faculty or action of producing mental images of what is not present or has not yet been experienced. Imagining something that is not immediately present to the senses often involves memory. Imagination is responsible for mental creative ability.

'Imagination is more important than knowledge' - *Albert Einstein*

o0o

An Analogy

Imagine you have just acquired the latest, the most stylish computer ever built. After unwrapping it, what is the first thing you have to do?

Plug it in, of course.

So **it has to be connected to a power supply**. There must be a power supply; it has to be connected either directly to the mains or to batteries. **There are no exceptions.**

Then the next stage: it has to be **turned on.** If it's not turned on it won't work - agreed?

Then it has to be registered. You have to show you own it, often by providing a password, that's a code that only you and the computer know. This makes your computer different from someone else's; your password helps to make it personal and helps you to connect.

4

So you have plugged it in, turned it on and registered your password. So far so good; but it still doesn't do anything, does it? At least, not until you have connected it to a program. If that program is to connect you to the internet then **WOW**! Now you are connected to all the world's computers, you can email, you have access to all the accumulated knowledge stored on what is sometimes called 'the information super-highway'. You can 'surf the net'. And all this is connected through a telephone, via cables, transmitters, aerial dishes and even satellites out in space.

NOW YOU'RE IN BUSINESS!

See a connection ... ?
    Plugged in ... the Candle
      Turned on ... the Crystal
        The Password ... Imagination
          The Internet ... the Mind

The Subconscious

There seems a gold mine within all of us from which we can extract everything we need in order to live life to the full. It's a miracle-working power that's found in the mind, but more importantly in the subconscious - maybe the last place most people would look. You don't need to acquire it; you already have it. Learn how to use it, understand it. Through the power of the subconscious mind you can attract all the wealth you'll ever need, and the freedom to be, to do, and to go as your heart desires. You can attract the ideal companion, as well as the right business associate or partners. Through it, you can even find the right buyer for your house. Though invisible, its power is real. Within your subconscious mind, and more importantly within the imagination, you will find the solution for every problem or worry, discover the cause for every effect.

To stand any chance of succeeding with our wishes or prayers, we have to have a method for understanding. It's the same as the relationship between a program and a computer. To help to understand what I mean, let's look at the relationship between hypnosis and the subconscious mind. Hypnosis, as understood by many psychologists, might be described as a state of excessive **suggestibility** in which a person seems to temporarily relinquish all conscious control of their behaviour. It seems they accept without question suggestions which in the conscious world they would recognise as blatantly irrational. Examples of this can be seen in the totally irrational behaviour of subjects at hypnotist stage shows.

Did you know that if you suggest to a person under hypnosis that the ice cube you have just placed in their hand is actually a burning ember, the subconscious mind, believing this to be true, will in fact produce a blister?

It's not unlike the placebo effect: a patient is given what they think is medicine, but which in fact is not; yet, remarkably, some people are cured. Think about it ... it's based on a lie, and yet manages to have the desired effect! The mind is truly amazing. To give you, the reader, the chance to experience this power for yourselves, let's try an experiment, using a pendulum.

A Pendulum
In my book *Discover Why Crystal Healing Works*, I use pictures. One such picture shows a young woman who can also look very old, a little like a witch. Another shows a staircase that moves as you look at it. The front cover of my book shows an obelisk: when you look straight at it you can see only hieroglyphics written along it, but if you tilt your head you can see a word. These effects can be quite disturbing if you are not aware of what is happening. But remember: in all cases the effect is being shown to you to help you understand the power you hold within your mind. This technique is a very powerful, effective way of exciting the imagination, which in my opinion holds the key. I will now show you how to use a pendulum to produce the same effect as the pictures.

o0o

'When imagination and willpower are in conflict, imagination will always win.'

o0o

Get a weight and tie it onto the end of a piece of string, so as to be able to use it like a pendulum. I have found that a simple key, like a Yale key, works just as well. You may have a crystal pendulum; this is even better. Now get a piece of paper, say A4 size, and draw a circle on it using a small saucer. Next, around the circumference put four dots, as if you where marking out a clock at twelve, three, six and nine o'clock. Then connect the dots making a cross; the point where the lines cross is the centre of the circle, and it's going to be a target. Place the paper on a table, sit down, and make yourself comfortable.

Hold the pendulum over the centre of the target. Steady it, if you have to, by allowing the pendulum to touch base, then lifting it just a little so that it is able to swing freely under the influence only of gravity. If you are uncomfortable, place your elbows onto the table to help support your arms. Whatever you do, **DO NOT MOVE.** Now, using only the power of you mind, imagine the pendulum swinging from side to side - and it will do so. Or imagine it swinging back to front, or swinging in a circular motion either clockwise or anticlockwise. If it's not going in the direction you want, then imagine it changing direction and it will. It may be slow at the beginning. But it will change, and you will get better at it with practice. Try it - I know you'll be astounded. Remember, I am only showing you this effect to help you understand the principles behind a wish kit.

A Letter
A useful analogy could be: Imagine you are going to send a letter. First you have to address it. You then have to put a stamp on it, and finally you have to post it. After that, you have to trust it will be delivered. Consider the effort that has to go into sending it, say, to the other side of town, and compare that with the effort required to send it half-way round the world - but for you, you only need to post it, so don't worry about the HOW, just know it happens.

Wishful thinking
Don't confuse all this with wishful thinking. Wishing with the aid of a wish kit is more controlled and more precise. There is a method. In the church they call it prayer. The power of prayer, if you have never experienced it, can be awesome, but it's not exclusive to a church, although it can certainly be found there. If you change the expression 'prayer power' to 'the power of thought', you start to get the idea of just

what could be involved in delivering your wishes, as in the case of the letter.

As with the analogy of the letter, we all know that sometimes it seems to take ages for a letter or postcard to arrive. Some take a relatively short time, whilst others can take weeks. It may take a while for your wish to come true, depending on the wish or prayer. Within 30 days could be described as average. Some suggest the timing is linked to the cycle of the moon. You may object it could take 30 days for your wish to come to fruition.

I remember one wish or prayer took 18 months. However, it was well worth the wait when it did finally arrive.

Part of the method you'll read about is 'visualisation'. A key element of this is, **be very precise**. To give you an idea, I will tell you a true story and you can judge for yourselves whether the wish was, in this case, fulfilled.

A Sports Car
I was told about a man who tried out a visualisation technique: he physically went along to a Mercedes garage and collected many brochures on their 350 sports car range. He sat in the car to see how it would feel. He could smell the newness of the leather. He then found the best picture he could, in a metallic blue, and proceeded to cut it out, then went to his car and stuck the picture behind the sun visor. Every time he got into the car he would deliberately touch the picture lovingly and imagine the smell of the leather, until this just became a habit. Although after a while the energy had gone out of it, he still did the action of touching the picture every time he got into his car. Now here's the twist: a very good friend of his went out and bought the very same car, same model, same colour. His friend had never mentioned he was interested in this type of car. When the man went out with his friend, he found himself in the car, the very same one he had been imagining, even down to the smell of the leather ... well, was his dream, his wish, answered? Not quite - so be precise!

The Modus Operandi of Wishes

Start by mentally slowing down: take a deep breath, relax, and just let go.

Take a white sheet of paper (A4 will do), or a clean white hanky, and place it on a table in front of you. After a moment, when you feel quite relaxed, place a candle onto a saucer or small plate (to protect your table from the heat), Then place the saucer on your paper or cloth and light it. Use the suggested colour of candle, depending on your wish (see page 10). If you haven't got a coloured candle then use a white one; a simple, inexpensive nightlight will do. Now you are **plugged in**.

Now, having chosen the appropriate Crystal or Gemstone (refer to page 15), take it and place it gently between you and the candle. You are now **turned on**.

Next, take the appropriate colour of paper (postcard size is ideal) and write out your wish or prayer - this is to be done between you and the Crystal (see example of wishes on page 13). This represents your **password**; you are making it personal.

Then take the Crystal or Gemstone and wrap it up carefully. Turn it in to a little parcel. Write a word or two on it to describe your wish, for example: Love, Health, Friendship, Wealth, Luck, Peace, or just A Wish. Now place it by a window, to allow it to 'see out'. This represents **the internet**.

Then say a prayer of thanks, such as: 'Divine Mother, Father, Higher Self, Guides and Angels, thank you for granting my wish,' or 'For the good and love of all, thank you for ...' Remember to say it as if you have already received your wish. Not 'I hope' or 'if'; say '**I have**', in the past tense.

Now visualise the wish granted. See its fulfilment in your mind's eye, and then imagine how you will feel when it comes about. **Energise it**.

Finally, blow out the candle, and wait a moment. You have just sent a kind of spiritual e-mail. Leave your wish in the parcel for up to 30 days and then you can retrieve the crystal, cleanse it, and it can be used again. Save the paper as a record of you wishes. Why not make a special box? It all helps to excite the imagination; and with the help of your imagination, you can move mountains.

Colour

Colour is important as a source of power. You may think it is stating the obvious to say that colour must be one of the greatest pleasures of life, although we probably all take it for granted. See the wonder of a sunset or the breaking of a new dawn, the splendour of clear night sky with a full moon, and the brilliance of the millions of stars. These things bring excitement to our senses and refreshment to our spirits. That's why it helps to boost the power of our wishes by using coloured paper for our wish or prayer.

**When powered by the energy of strong intention,
universal law becomes activated.**

There is currently no explanation that sits easily within the parameters of conventional science to explain how these things seem to work. There again, science can't explain the placebo effect despite accepting and recognising that it exists.

To help make your wishes come true, this exclusive 'Rosewood Wish Kit' draws from an ancient knowledge that's almost magical like, and yet seems so desperately needed in today's modern world. The following pages are divided into seven categories. Below, the appropriate colour of paper is given for each category. White can be used as an alternative for all the groups.

Category	Colour of paper	Colour of candle
Love	Red	Red
Health	Orange	Orange
Friendship	Yellow	Yellow
Wealth	Green	Green
Luck	Blue	Blue
Peace	White	White
Any Wish	Lilac	Lilac

The following are just some ideas on how to formulate a wish. You could write out, for example: *In the name of Love, I thank you for granting my Wish for.....*

LOVE	*finding my new partner*
HEALTH	*curing my illness.*
FRIENDSHIP	*sending a special friend*
WEALTH	*winning the lottery.*
LUCK	*finding my lost... ....*
PEACE	*giving me understanding*
ANY WISH	*the child soon to be born*

Ask most people about their goals - what they would like to be in, say, five years' time; how much money they want to have, what they want to be doing at work, at home or at play - and most will say they don't know. The truth is that most people don't. This is one of the most common responses and also one of the major reasons why people seem to fail.

In the Bible - Mark 11:24 - it is written: 'Believe that you **HAVE** received it', and not 'Believe that you **WILL** receive it'.

According to this piece of the Scriptures, we can receive a thing by believing we already have it, that it's already ours. This is why we make our affirmations, our prayers, our wishes in the present tense.

The following ideas are to help you focus on, and formulate, your own specific wish or prayer.

Ideas for Goals
To increase net worth (exact amount of invested capital)
To be self-determined, and allow others the same right
To increase income (exact amount should be stated)
To gain maximum energy easily, for use at will
To have warm and loving human relationships
To relax fully at will and avoid tensions
To increase overall self-concept
To stop all destructive criticism
To be responsible for yourself
To achieve a happy marriage

Remember, the best way to formulate a wish, or prayer, is to write it down so that when you read it back it makes sense and is affirmative, in the **past tense**. For example, if you wanted to attract a new partner, as mentioned in the 'love' section, then this is how you could go about doing it.

Find a piece of red paper and write on it your wish or prayer, in this case: *In the name of love, thank you for granting my wish and bringing me my new partner.*

Fold the paper around any of the crystals mentioned for love: Rose Quarts, Amethyst or Carnelian. Turn it into a little parcel; then write on it 'LOVE', and place it in the window.

Then come back to your lit candle and say a prayer of thanks, for example: 'Divine Mother, Father, Higher Self, Guides and Angels, thank you for granting me my wish (or Prayer).' Or: 'God the Father, in the name of your Son our Lord Jesus Christ, thank you for granting me my prayer (or wish).'

Find the way that is comfortable for you. If it feels right, then it probably is right. Trust your instincts - they have been developed over many thousands of years.

Next, imagine how you would feel if the wish or prayer you have just made is granted. Feel it ... imagine it ... energise it ... and then let go. Take a moment, then blow out the candle. You have now disconnected yourself from a very powerful mental exercise - a little like when you disconnect your computer from the internet.

In church, it would be called a prayer. It really doesn't seem to matter whether you are religious or not; the facts seem to be that when help or assistance is required, then a universal life force, often called God, will help us to succeed, wherever possible - you only have to ask.

o0o

'For everyone who asks, receives; he who seeks, finds; and to him who knocks, the door will be opened.'
Matthew 7:7-8

o0o

Some further ideas that may help to create or formulate your wish or prayer:

For ...Love
>To keep a true love
>To charm the partner of your dreams
>To mend a broken friendship
>To attract a new partner
>To create a happy relationship
>To arouse sexual passions
>To find a soul mate
>To put life back into a relationship

For ...Health
>To stop headaches and migraines
>To improve memory and concentration
>To cure an illness
>To gain greater vitality
>To remove aches and pains
>To overcome anxiety
>To avoid panic attacks
>To become pregnant

For ...Friendship
>To increase your circle of friends
>To attract a true friend
>To know you're loved
>To share love with someone else
>To find strength to support a friend at a time of crisis
>To find a way to comfort a friend who is suffering
>To forgive and be forgiven
>To mend a broken friendship

For ...Wealth
>To acquire money and wealth
>To win contests, lotteries and at cards
>To change luck for the better
>To attract a new business or offer of work
>To become self-employed
>To get back into work
>To attract golden opportunities
>To be promoted

For ...Luck
To find a new home
To succeed in business
To always attract good fortune
To always be on the winning side
To be in the right place at the right time
To be lucky in love
To find the right partner, both in business and in love
To always arrive safely

For...Peace
To acquire peace of mind
To always be in control
To gain freedom from any doubt
To gain self-confidence
To keep a home in balance
To change sorrow to joy
To always travel safely
To have a faith

For ...Any Wish
To start a family
To avoid trouble
To gain new insights
To forget the past
To end loneliness
To have the wisdom to make the right decisions
To improve a poor business
To overcome depression

o0o

**If you knew you could have anything you imagined
What would you imagine?**

o0o

To help choose your special crystal, the one that can help your wish, a list taken from my various books is provided below.

For Love ... Rose Quartz, Amethyst or Carnelian.

For Health ... Carnelian, Red Jasper or Rock Crystal.

For Friendship ... Moonstone, Carnelian or Amethyst.

For Wealth ... Green Aventurine, Hematite or Tiger Eye.

For Luck ... Obsidian snowflake, Green Aventurine or Moonstone.

For Peace ... Green Aventurine, Rose Quartz or Rhodonite.

Just a few Crystals and Gemstones with some further suggestions that may help in providing a focal point for wishes:

Jasper: A powerful healing stone with renowned mystical powers. In astrology, represents Aries, the first energy of the cycle of life.

Rose Quartz: Renowned for working wonders on aches and pains. A healer and a love stone.

Black Onyx: For willpower, helps with losing weight or giving up smoking. Instils calm and serenity, diminishes depression.

Mother of Pearl: Aptly dubbed 'the sea of tranquillity', calms the nerves and creates physical harmony.

Tiger Eye: Forget your worries with this stress-busting stone. A confidence stone, fights hypochondria.

Carnelian: Adults only, a stone for nights of love and passion. A friendly one, a highly evolved healer.

Green Aventurine: Well known as a money magnet. Acts as a general tonic on a physical level.

Rhodonite: Improves your memory and helps revive youthful yearnings. Calms the nerves and reduces stress.

Sodalite: Brings back the joys of spring, helps impart youth and freshness. Calms and clears the mind.

Obsidian Snowflake: A lucky talisman, and a bringer of good luck and fortune. Favoured by ancient Mexican cultures to neutralise negative magic.

Blue Agate: A super charger that gives energy and vitality. Improves the ego. A stone of strength and courage.

Amethyst: A love stone. Attracts love, helps to find that special partner. A romantic stone, also aids creative thinking and relieves insomnia.

Hematite: An optimistic inspirer of courage, magnetism and strength. Lifts gloominess and depression.

Rock Crystal: Increases the healing power, whilst boosting your energy field. Holds a place of unique importance in the world of Gems. Increases the powers of other minerals.

Moonstone: A fertility stone for extra help when starting a family. A good emotional balancer and solid friend, inspiring wisdom; a very lucky, sacred Gem.

o0o

Jesus said,
Everything is possible for him who believes.

Mark 9:23

o0o

Remember, a wish kit needs its tools just as Clark Kent needed a costume to complete his transformation into Superman. Our wish kit needs as its costume a candle, a crystal and the imagination of the mind. There is a simple truth about ourselves and the world we live in, and it is simply to *believe*. Keep an open mind. Belief pulls back the blinds of illusion and allows us to see the truth. This then carves a direct pathway into our inner world, where all our needs can be found.

o0o

See your local stockist for any Gemstones and Crystals mentioned in this publication.

However, if you are having difficulty in obtaining any of the stones mentioned, we do offer our own mail order service and would be more than pleased to supply any of the stones listed.

Most Gemstones and Crystals, with just a few exceptions - for example Mother of Pearl - can be supplied in the form of Tumblestones. These are smooth, rounded stones ideal for use as a Birthstone or as Healing Crystals. The nature of Mother of Pearl, and one or two others, prevents them being supplied as Tumblestones; however, we would be pleased to supply these in their natural form.

For further details - write to:
ROSEWOOD
P.O. Box 219, Huddersfield, West Yorkshire. HD2 2YT

E-mail enquiries to: info@rosewood-gifts.co.uk

Or why not visit our website for even more information:

www.rosewood-gifts.co.uk

Other titles in the 'POWER FOR LIFE' series:

Discover your own Special Birthstone and the renowned Healing Powers of Crystals REF. (BK1) A look at Birthstones, personality traits and characteristics associated with each Sign of the Zodiac – plus a guide to the author's own unique range of Power Gems.

A Special Glossary of Healing Stones plus Birthstones REF. (BK2) An introduction to Crystal Healing, with an invaluable Glossary listing common ailments and suggesting combinations of Gemstones/Crystals.

Gemstone & Crystal Elixirs – Potions for Love, Health, Wealth, Energy and Success REF. (BK4) An ancient form of 'magic', invoking super-natural powers. You won't believe the power you can get from a drink!

Crystal Pendulum for Dowsing REF. (BK5) An ancient knowledge for unlocking your Psychic Power, to seek out information not easily available by any other means. Contains easy-to-follow instructions.

Crystal Healing – Fact or Fiction? Real or Imaginary? REF. (BK6) Find the answer in this book. Discover a hidden code used by Jesus Christ for healing, and read about the science of light and colour. It's really amazing.

How to Activate the Hidden Power in Gemstones and Crystals REF. (BK7) The key is to energise the thought using a crystal. The conscious can direct – but discover the real power. It's all in this book.

Astrology: The Secret Code REF. (BK8) In church it's called 'Myers Briggs typology'. In this book it's called 'psychological profiling'. If you read your horoscope, you need to read this to find your true birthstone.

Talismans, Charms and Amulets REF. (BK9) Making possible the powerful transformations which we would not normally feel empowered to do without a little extra help. Learn how to make a lucky talisman.

A Guide to the Mysteries surrounding Gemstones & Crystals REF. (BK10) Crystal healing, birthstones, crystal gazing, lucky talismans, elixirs, crystal dowsing, astrology, rune stones, amulets and rituals.

A Simple Guide to Gemstone & Crystal Power – a mystical A-Z of stones REF. (BK11) From Agate to Zircon, all you ever needed or wanted to know about the mystical powers of gemstones and crystals.

Change Your Life by Using the Most Powerful Crystal on Earth REF. (BK12) The most powerful crystal on earth can be yours. A book so disarmingly simple to understand, yet with a tremendous depth of knowledge.

All the above books are available from your local stockist,
or, if not, from the publisher.

NOTES

Welcome to the world of Rosewood

An extract from a 'thank- you' letter for one of my books.

"I realised just how much you really had indeed understood me and my need for direction and truly have allowed me the confidence and strength to know and believe I can achieve whatever I want in life"

If you like natural products, hand-crafted gifts including Gemstone jewellery, objects of natural beauty – the finest examples from Mother Nature, tinged with an air of Mystery – then we will not disappoint you. For those who can enjoy that feeling of connection with the esoteric nature of Gemstones and Crystals, then our 'Power for Life – Power Bracelets could be ideal for you. Each bracelet comes with its own guide explaining a way of thinking that's so powerful it will change your life and the information comes straight from the Bible. e.g. read Mark 11: 22

We regularly give inspirational talks on Crystal Power – fact or fiction? A captivating story about the world's fascination with natural gemstones and crystals and how the Placebo effect explains the healing power of gemstones and crystals – it's intriguing. And it's available on a CD

To see our full range of books, jewellery and gifts including CD's and DVD'S

Visit our web site - www.rosewood-gifts.co.uk

To see our latest videos go to 'You Tube' and type in Rosewood Gifts.